SOFT TARGETS

Also by Deborah Landau

The Uses of the Body
The Last Usable Hour
Orchidelirium

SOFT TARGETS
DEBORAH LANDAU

Copper Canyon Press
Port Townsend, Washington

Copper Canyon Press is in residence at Fort Worden State Park in Port Townsend, Washington, under the auspices of Centrum. Centrum is a gathering place for artists and creative thinkers from around the world, students of all ages and backgrounds, and audiences seeking extraordinary cultural enrichment.

LIBRARY OF CONGRESS CATALOGING-IN-PUBLICATION DATA

Names: Landau, Deborah, Ph.D., author.
Title: Soft targets / Deborah Landau.
Description: Port Townsend, Washington : Copper Canyon Press, [2019]
Identifiers: LCCN 2018036632 | ISBN 9781556595660 (pbk. : alk. paper)
Classification: LCC PS3612.A54755 A6 2019 | DDC 811/.6—dc23
LC record available at https://lccn.loc.gov/2018036632

9 8 7 6 5 4 3 2 first printing

Copper Canyon Press
Post Office Box 271
Port Townsend, Washington 98368

for Ethan, Julian,
and Miranda

ACKNOWLEDGMENTS

Thank you to the editors of the following publications, in which versions of poems from this collection originally appeared: Academy of American Poets Poem-a-Day, *The American Poetry Review*, *Boston Review*, *Freeman's*, *Green Mountains Review*, *The Literary Review*, *The New Yorker*, and *Poetry*.

"there were real officers in the streets" first appeared in *Resistance, Rebellion, Life: 50 Poems Now* (Knopf).

I am grateful to the Guggenheim Foundation for providing invaluable support during the writing of this book.

Warmest thanks to Catherine Barnett, Alex Dimitrov, John Freeman, Peter Nickowitz, Meghan O'Rourke, Michael Wiegers, and Matthew Zapruder. Much gratitude always to everyone at Copper Canyon Press. And to Mark, my love

CONTENTS

SOFT TARGETS

when it comes to this fleshed neck

~

When it comes to this fleshed neck
even a finger could do it

even a sharp stick,
a blunt blow, a fall—

my jugular
there's a soft target

and night is a soft target
all of us within it

Osama shot dead
in his pajamas

and everyone
on the Brooklyn-bound F

as a man removes a bomb
from his bag

a square of chocolate
he detonates in his mouth

there were real officers in the streets

(Paris)

~

There were real officers in the streets
but they were doing it wrong.

One winked at me, another was purely conceptual,
one thought to himself as I walked by, *you little bitch.*

Bulge-knobs of their guns made them aural,
made them real big *machismo,*

even the skinny ones, even the abstract.
A certain beauty in the duty of it.

Meanwhile he was broken, she was concussed,
and we returned home, gilded with what, safety?

In advance of danger
animals agitate.

When the time comes all this
will be only shouts and disturbance.

~

A breath leaves the body and wishes it could return
maybe, the news rich with failure, dither,
terror, the bloated moon in constant charge of us as vapor

and this did frame our constituency
even in our cozy homes, even in a painless state
on the downriver, O oblivion—

sipping champagne as another night brings forth,
dancing its big plan, its damage.
I had a thought but it turned autumn, turned cold.

I had a body, unwearied, vital, despite the funeral in everything—
ample with bodies, covered in graves and gardens, potholes and water,
an ardent river we walked together, a wine and rising breeze.

Much trouble at hand, yet the lilies still.

~

Still there was bread on the plate, still wine,
while the streets filled with refugees,

and the French stepped over them
en route to patisseries, cafés—

Massive powers that be
what will be?

We smoke our pipes
to forget you

and mildly now we bide our time,
the violence and real cities

under siege
but also filled this morning

with coffee drinkers, office workers,
taxi drivers, boys on bikes—

again we came to rest
on the riverbanks

finding a bloodlight
flooding what we'd come to see.

~

How is it to have a body today
to walk in this city, to run?

To be strong and whole in daylight
is to be tapped perhaps for a blade

yet off into the air we're sent
in flesh and kismet it is

if we're in the right or wrong or right
school, office, market, concert, café.

Red velvet cells, the elemental oxygen
and pall of eyelids, fists, feet,

vivid apparitions of those who have jumped or fallen
in the jingle of no spring.

Existence is killing us.
I don't want to see what can't be unseen.

Nights we play the game of going to sleep,
expecting to wake up.

~

O you who want to slaughter us,
we'll be dead soon enough, what's the rush—
and this our only world.

As you can see it has a problem,
as you can see the citizens are hanging heavy,
the citizens' minds are out.

Eros, Eros, in Paris we stayed all night
in a seraphic cocktail haze
despite the blacked-out theater, the shuttered panes.

Tonight we're the most tender of soft targets,
pulpy with alcohol and all asloth.
Monsieur, can we get a few more?

There are unmistakable signs of trouble,
but we have days and days still.
Let's be giddy, maybe.

Time lights a little fire.
We are animal hungry
down to our intricate bones.

O beautiful habits of living,
let me dwell on you awhile.

~

Summer seemed to hover
along the Seine

as we sat with our backs
to the street letting time pass,

lying all afternoon in the grass
as if green and insect were the world.

I am, I am, and you are, you are,
we wrote, until the paper seemed a tree again

and we walked beneath it
greener and unsullied afresh.

Golden we were
in the moment of conception

and alive, as if
we always would be.

~

It was good getting drunk in the undulant city,
whiskey lopping off the day's fear—

dawn came with an element of Xanax,
dusk came and I dumbed myself down.

Where there were brides, grooms,
these bored boysoldiers with iPhones and guns.

I'm a soft target, you're a soft target,
and the city has a hundred hundred thousand softs;

the pervious skin, the softness of the face,
the wrist inners, the hips, the lips, the tongue,

the global body,
its infinite permutable softnesses—

soft targets, soft readers, drinkers,
pedestrians in rain;

in the failing light we walked out
and now we share a room with it

(would you like to read to me in the soft
would you like to enter me in the soft

would you like a lunch of me in the soft
in its long delirium?)

The good news is we have each other.
The bad news is Kalashnikov assault rifles,

submachine guns, pistols, ammunition,
four boxes packed with thousands of small steel balls.

~

The morning world in crisp relief—

clotheslines, windowsills, sunflowers in sun

even after a night like that

even after the worst night

the Mediterranean sparkling obliviously

abandoned poussettes on the promenade

bodies on asphalt, a certain nausea of sound

beneath the streets inside the metros

up on the rooftops something is cooking

~

keep the doors
locked windows
closed coast clear
and don't be soft
at the airport, café,
club, restaurant,
concert, in church

(when shots
punctured the room
when explosions
smoked and clouded
he was all alive, spasmodic
like a fish in floodwaters she)

~

Let's resume.
It was a stifling summer
and marred by slaughter.

I rolled over and tried to sleep
thinking mostly of self-preservation,
how it makes everything else irrelevant,

follows us around the block
with its narrow anger
at the wild risk of it, all living things.

By which method
shall I become formless,
or reach a final form?

The odds constantly changing,
the moon a low smudge on black
and the roads all closed.

Soldiers pacing their new stations on the square
as if safety were calculable,
as if there were a plan.

~

And so we've become ourselves

again in the old style side by side

in fragility, beside the pantheon crypt

doing nothing as if for a reason.

We'll lose to gravity dark and pure

beyond what can be replenished beyond

what can be beyond, a plot of nerves gone under

(the musk scent and filthy pile we'll be).

But we were lustrous from time to time,

in a garden in a city in a wood melodious with pine.

Blur of speech in the gullet, gale of want in the throat.

Woke up warm tomorrow in a spot of sun.

A flesh. A wild alive all only.

those nazis, they knew what to do with a soft

(Frankfurt)

~

i don't know
what's so neo
about neo-nazis

they seem a lot
like the old
nazis to me

shouting *jews will not replace us*
in charlottesville
in frankfurt

marching by my grandmother's
house shouting
pretty much the same

ought we to get going now
galloping seems
a good idea

~

Frankfurt, 1938, Oma was a soft target
got her soft the fuck out of there

smuggled out her egg purse to become us
and so it ended and so it didn't end

(if she'd been distracted, if she'd lived blindly,
if she'd been dazed or dullard or out of luck)

kissed her dog goodbye, snuck candy
in her pockets, coins in her shoes

ran past the door of her school
her doctor's office

her favorite park, the house
where the boy she secretly loved lived—

was made to wade into the night like a swimmer
thought she could not swim

~

Those Nazis, they knew
what to do with a soft

we were just powder puffs
living ones

falling, falling, dandelion fluff

there went my family
there went yours

epic of soft prolonged
in a long fall

an adagio of soft

(meanwhile waltzing
meanwhile chocolate

bread, a lullaby
for their cherished *Kinder*

a goodnight story
a goodnight kiss)

~

She dreamed a train underwater
a door in the sea, an end—

even in a clean kitchen, even in a smart dress,
with friends and teachers, a brother

on the soccer team, the bright star
she shared with all Germans, the sun,

she wasn't in a good position,
not that night, not any night—

and when, how, when, would she
get to New York, St. Louis, Detroit?

(the swiftest bike to bike
a frantic Frankfurt, her wits,

the manifold papers
certified stamped correct)

~

Not me not mine not now
she thought
and bore away her family
with a winter wind
a vivid mind
with my mother
stitched inside her
snug and soundly now
carried off
through the oceanic
effluvium soft across the sea
she sewed a wedding dress
and it too was soft silk soft

~

Will we ever run out of days?
A new country, refuge,

a nuptial bed—
advance past the past

now, imperishable
despite history fragility fear

she went for it
and birthed a soft target

her mini-soft
dropped one spring

and she too was soft
too soft

the new body
plumping with blood

~

And now we know from Soft.

Pulse, you know it,
and History knows.

Over and over it sics
itself upon the soft.

Eat Drink Breathe
and Kiss your favorite face—

Do what you want
and now.

Soon laid deep beneath
the flimsy weeds we'll be

and how—

The last day
is the purest theft.

America wants it soft

~

This is my plangent note to the ambassadors of love.

(All dreaming now is retroactive.)

The radioactive someday is here.

Our kings are cranks, crooks, incongruous,

they are improper, ill equipped,

how is it we pushed the handle down and they popped out?

Toasted!

And now they sit at the head of our table,

can we be excused?

Scurrilous scumbags, X-rays of greed, they move themselves

up the flagpole, razing the trees.

~

To be female on coronation night was a difficulty.

Her skin under his thumb was a sickhouse was too much.

Our king no you aren't. Our king? Not at all.

Our king on paper our king in the spotlight

our king in the outflowing tide—

our king on my daughter?

His weight dropt in mid-night and stung her little bed.

A creep, a Porphyro, a flesh struggling to be man.

There was no excuse for the smug frog of him.

~

Comrades, commend yourselves

on a job very poorly done.

And now what will be? I'm alarmed.

Keep your passport handy, keep cash,

keep water and batteries, collect your meds

and loved ones, just in case,

and silence your phone.

Stay off the beach, the street, the planet—

There must be some mistake.

(And the doomsday clock flicks forward,

stares us down.)

~

Demanded their order in our courts
wore their crimes and misdemeanors
set their bears loose in our gardens
pled us guilty and said so
and said no and so again
desperate they were in general
ridiculous not sublime
this malignancy pumped up
ran deep and deeper into crime
no good our legs
no use religion or hope or signs,
this king was all he was cracked up to be
will boys be? Leave it all to he

~

Locked and loaded
fire and fury
the daft-master

bastard art of war
(otherwise known
as look I've got this

big bad prick
with which to blast
your astroturf)

I'll put one, two,
then three fingers
inside you, he said,

windows breaking
as the detonation
throbbed and shook

he stopped a moment
just planted on top
and melting there

that panicked thrumming
was the bomb
and such a dirty one

~

This viciousness, it makes me quiver.
Instead of a kiss, a ferocity—

> *do not look at the flash*
> *take shelter lie flat and cover your head*

A hostile city, hurting.
The stalks of flowers won't hold up

> *even if separated from your family*
> *stay where you are*

One person is mauled,
another eats a sandwich

> *do not call the school*
> *do not pick up your children*

The killing was not well done,
it was in planetary contempt and mindless

> *radiation cannot be seen, smelled*
> *get clean soon and gently wipe your ears*

Birds cruelpecking crumbs left in a pocket
in the glaringafter—

~

America wants it soft—
doesn't want to see

smashed we are
in mad simultaneity:

cat purring on the window seat
as the storm surge takes the boat,

kids scavenging cactuses
in Madagascar,

kings inhaling sea-urchin custard
at Eleven Madison Park,

the botanical lily opening in its humid garden
while, facing his worst emergency in blackest night,

the prisoner finds himself obliged
to be iced in darkness.

~

And what now of dreaming?

We've failed the planet has published our failures.

Our crimes are perpetual methane and sweltering, arrogant and endless—

poor fucks we are, breathing mindlessly as the marsh grass floods,

and here comes the supermoon again, like it's so special.

Weak and disordered become the governments, disquiet rules us now.

Onward, I thought, and so we were obscured.

The end of America, no one knew how to manage it

but we tried the typical ways of numbing pain—

my daughter painted tiny flowers on her toenails,

I mixed honey and vodka, squeezing in a lime,

and we carried on with our breathing—

my father was still alive, my body kept aging,

the pills helped a little, not a lot.

into the sheets we slipped, a crisis

~

Into the sheets we slipped, a crisis

affixing us to each other again and again.

Womb was I, turned out.

The babies were a transcript of our making,

a panorama of life on its back.

Thrice I plunked out the humans,

until we'd had enough of such extravagant weather

and lay there thinking of the bed,

how much of life happens there

At the center of everything the piquant transitory joy

and from this even the charred wrecks,

even the dahmers nazis bin ladens all flesh

fleshed out of wild unmanageable Eros

(we're always a bit dirty with it)

~

In the birth room you couldn't think,
you were a single moan and tangle,

you were an agony, maybe,
but also had wings like never before.

Welcome to the love bazaar,
let's dip back into it again, virility!

Pheromonal lure of silk slipping off skin,
excessive again his kiss, her shudder,

as snow petals down a lace of white flowers
and our baby sleeps in her indigo crib.

Such a reckless act, to pop out a human,
with the jaws of the world set to kill.

~

And she arrived before dawn, staring straight—
her job: to eat what exists.

Any caress is precious, exaltation
in the breathing room, a life force—

who knew our brushstrokes had been so precise,
greening darkness with this young vine,

and this new pain, to slow time—
drew more and more from the nub of her

until she was herself,
emerged ready to live her one life

and she seemed friendly,
looking sideways as I swiped her clean.

Honey, here are your limbs,
we are not too late.

~

beyond the edge of field, the border of photograph—

in flux floating attached only to one another

three vanishing figures

a lullaby, though elsewhere famine

elsewhere flame

gleaming they come to us from nothing what now

~

Daughter is a soft target,
in a fuchsia crush she's come

bare and guileless, fair and free,
funneling forward without a helmet

toward the barest sickest tree—
(keep them from being head-kicked-in,

keep their blood inside, intact,
keep them from shooting sprees,

from X-rays and MRSA,
spiked metal, sadistic men).

Take a self and put her out
in the wood for the struggle.

Invest in armature.

~

In the cut of Mercy she's in my arms;

in the cut of Cruelty she's done

a blood slump on the subway floor.

Can we live this way?

I think someone has done grave injury.

I think person or persons—

I think we're losing by default.

Slaughter happened around the planet;

we stayed in the thicket whipping up love.

~

Yet all this time we have been alive.
The charms of the present
aren't lost on me, Marcel,

as past the guard into school we walk
through a deafening rainstorm
that has nothing to do with wars.

Did dragons live when the dinosaurs were alive?
Soft asks, her childhood swishing by
in its rapture of plenitude.

All afternoon she lies on her back
staring at the void,
but to her it's just the sky.

Oh this life for a while so dreamy
we wake eager to be in it
and sleep imperfectly delivers us

to a buttery layer of jam on toast
in this best of all possible worlds
to cultivate in the aftermath our gardens—

still here and portioned out to us now.

~

Someone's put potted orchids in the mammography waiting room.

For hope maybe, for promise of bloom, a violet refusal to refuse—

and hung a mirror in the cubicle, the better to admire by

while changing into the pepto-gown.

Look! my mammary glands awaiting their mammogram,

plush with milk last year, now stilled

in advance of the smashing slab.

A mammogram gives the coldest ultimatum:

soft targets in your skin-socks prepare for a flattening,

and prolonging everything my lungs, this persistent heart,

as the day's pain spatulas in on the twitter feed

Aleppo Jerusalem London Kabul

violence accumulating in windows on a screen.

~

Mama was a target in her transplant bed
where she *I found myself praying*
as the chemicals daisied in, pinpricks, a salvation

the door to the hall was not for her
walking was not for her
then breathing was not

being lifted aloft that was
and a stretcher and a still still bed

a faraway face was she by then
with no further questions
with a difficulty turning on the light

did she fall soft that last night
(and now?)

afar afar she went my soft star

the silence will be sudden then last

~

We rocked it for a while in New York

it seemed like quite the era

and had the martinis to prove it

many magnificents

but the footlights were shining too brightly now

was our time past?

We're not in our coffinclothes, not yet

Don't mope, Mother would say

(but I'm so very good at it!)

On the other hand

I'm feeling kinda good today in my ginny way

and bought myself some cocktails

and thought of the planet wheel

and how one might

hop off

~

I'll antioxidize as best I can
bat away death with berries and flax
but there's no surviving
this slick merciless world
a bucket of guts we'll be
full-blown dead
though why wax gloomy
we're not real
just a pudding of flesh
trying gamely to preserve ourselves
my ducky grandee, glowing friend
let's sing a bit   this may end
in love may end in blood
but it will   (badly) end

~

Sybaritic afterlife I don't crave you.
I like daylight, I like crowds,
I don't think it will be charming underground.
The silence will be sudden then last—

what's chic will shrink,
there won't be any pretty, pity,
will never peaches there, or air,
we'll be so squashed and sour there.

I don't want a cold place,
don't want a threadbare
clamp and consequence all old.
Our loneliness will be prolonged then go too far.

Oh fuck it's true,
then nothing left of you.

~

Has it turned out we've wasted our time?
We've wasted our time.

Our magnificent bodies on the dissecting table,
our day after tomorrow,
our what to do now.

The stink of us so undignified—
the endgame of bloom.

We will lose the sun,
struck and disassembled
lightly down and crawling like a worm.

This earth it is a banquet and laid on its table we—
a puncture in the wound room, crude and obvious.

The raving lunatics they are upon us,
but we are raving too.

the snow goes to the gallows of a warm grass and what survives

~

The deepest redress is a thick and fulsome snow.
Peaceful prevail of afternoon, looking out
at this bluish marvel the air.

The snow realizes you a body, puts on you a hat,
tombs you in its second nature, with consequence
of sepia, a leaking dusky blue.

The snow fumbles at your borders,
wants a way in.

In the snow we are angelic
and it's not discouraging in fact it is marvelous
when the snow has its arms around us
and we walk the streets as if safe.

You're a child, even in midlife.
The snow clouds us in peppery breath
and the air comes fresh.

It comes and goes and comes again,
it doesn't aim for durability
it accumulates for the sake of it
and doesn't want to last.

The snow, I envy it,
it will vanish
but it doesn't care,

it's its own garden,
its own cool chalky paint—
kicks up
an alabaster splendor

then retreats without complaint.

~

As if it were a heaven:

the snow my subject!
my pristine—

what girl doesn't want to lie down in it.

The snow has a thin mouth,
it has a salve in it, the snow,

I hereby nominate it for my favorite embroidery,
it is so many things

(there's no surviving this storm—
even the snow won't survive it, and it *is* the storm)

~

The snow goes to the gallows
of a warm grass and what survives?

Seasons grow immodest,
the bullet sun does parch

and drive us migratory
in search of new and fertile fields.

The long drought makes blaze the plankton
makes smoke the oceans

and insincere the governments—
a demise indelicate.

We're in a deep jelly now
no cause for applause

but try a little clemency
my body is warm today, and yours,

we have this small span of time
and in this way we're millionaires.

Bright colors we make when pressed, see?
Basta! dawdling on the edge again that's me.

~

So I told the sky it should stay blue

told my daughter she should stay breathing

told my love he should and we would

as the monster storms showed their teeth

and the fires flared and the wines

weren't plum enough to numb us

and our leaders' virulent egos seethed

(people dying off as if it were nothing

to leave this planet as if it were a breeze)

don't blame the wisteria

~

Don't blame the wisteria for setting off a feeling like freedom a feeling like joy.

We watched the people walking in the open square—

one of them was a specialist in killing, fear was the way of others.

I've seen the most extraordinary thing about people, their faces.

Remember the trees in springtime, we ate candy beneath them,

shouts from the playground, static of yellowjackets, your fresh new haircut.

Here's a tweeted canto, some words for the end of the world—

for when I am forever nothing, and you are

(and you and you).

What we were for such a brief.

(M with the laundry, the dog at his bowl, the boys going at it out back.)

O you who want to slaughter us, we'll be dead soon enough what's the rush

and this our only world.

Now bring me a souvenir from the desecrated city,

something tender, something that might bloom.

NOTES

pages 15–16: The last three lines draw from Aurelien Breeden and Lilia Blaise's "Frenchman Plotting 'Imminent' Attack Is Charged with Terrorism," *New York Times*, March 30, 2016.

page 38: The italicized lines are from *In Case of Emergency: Preparing for an Imminent Missile Threat* (Guam's Joint Information Center Fact Sheet).

ABOUT THE AUTHOR

Deborah Landau is the author of four collections of poetry. Her work has appeared in *The American Poetry Review*, *The Best American Poetry*, *The New Yorker*, *The New York Times*, *The Paris Review*, *Poetry*, *Tin House*, and *The Wall Street Journal*. In 2016 she was awarded a Guggenheim Fellowship. She teaches in and directs the creative writing program at New York University and lives in Brooklyn with her family.

Lannan Literary Selections

For two decades Lannan Foundation has supported the publication and distribution of exceptional literary works. Copper Canyon Press gratefully acknowledges their support.

LANNAN LITERARY SELECTIONS 2019

Jericho Brown, *The Tradition*

Deborah Landau, *Soft Targets*

Paisley Rekdal, *Nightingale*

Natalie Scenters-Zapico, *Lima :: Limón*

Matthew Zapruder, *Father's Day*

RECENT LANNAN LITERARY SELECTIONS FROM
COPPER CANYON PRESS

Sherwin Bitsui, *Dissolve*

Marianne Boruch, *Cadaver, Speak*

John Freeman, *Maps*

Jenny George, *The Dream of Reason*

Ha Jin, *A Distant Center*

Deborah Landau, *The Uses of the Body*

Maurice Manning, *One Man's Dark*

Rachel McKibbens, *blud*

W. S. Merwin, *The Lice*

Aimee Nezhukumatathil, *Oceanic*

Camille Rankine, *Incorrect Merciful Impulses*

Paisley Rekdal, *Imaginary Vessels*

Brenda Shaughnessy, *So Much Synth*

Frank Stanford, *What About This: Collected Poems of Frank Stanford*

Ocean Vuong, *Night Sky with Exit Wounds*

C.D. Wright, *Casting Deep Shade*

Javier Zamora, *Unaccompanied*

Ghassan Zaqtan (translated by Fady Joudah), *The Silence That Remains*

Poetry is vital to language and living. Since 1972, Copper Canyon Press has published extraordinary poetry from around the world to engage the imaginations and intellects of readers, writers, booksellers, librarians, teachers, students, and donors.

WE ARE GRATEFUL FOR THE MAJOR SUPPORT PROVIDED BY:

THE PAUL G. ALLEN
FAMILY FOUNDATION

4
CULTURE

Lannan

ART WORKS.
National
Endowment
for the Arts
arts.gov

A&
OFFICE OF ARTS & CULTURE
——— SEATTLE ———

 WASHINGTON STATE
ARTS COMMISSION

TO LEARN MORE ABOUT UNDERWRITING
COPPER CANYON PRESS TITLES,
PLEASE CALL 360-385-4925 EXT. 103

WE ARE GRATEFUL FOR THE MAJOR SUPPORT PROVIDED BY:

Anonymous

Jill Baker and Jeffrey Bishop

Anne and Geoff Barker

Donna and Matt Bellew

John Branch

Diana Broze

Sarah and Tim Cavanaugh

Beatrice R. and Joseph A. Coleman Foundation

Laurie and Oskar Eustis

Mimi Gardner Gates

Linda Gerrard and Walter Parsons

Nancy Gifford

Gull Industries Inc. on behalf of Ruth and William True

The Trust of Warren A. Gummow

Phil Kovacevich and Eric Wechsler

Lakeside Industries Inc. on behalf of Jeanne Marie Lee

Maureen Lee and Mark Busto

Rhoady Lee and Alan Gartenhaus

Ellie Mathews and Carl Youngmann as The North Press

Anne O'Donnell and John Phillips

Petunia Charitable Fund and adviser Elizabeth Hebert

Gay Phinney

Suzie Rapp and Mark Hamilton

Emily and Dan Raymond

Jill and Bill Ruckelshaus

Kim and Jeff Seely

Richard Swank

University Research Council of DePaul University

Vincentian Endowment Foundation

Dan Waggoner

Barbara and Charles Wright

Caleb Young and Keep It Cinematic

The dedicated interns and faithful volunteers of Copper Canyon Press

The Chinese character for poetry is made up of two parts:
"word" and "temple." It also serves as pressmark for
Copper Canyon Press.

The poems are set Adobe Caslon Pro.
Book design and composition by Phil Kovacevich.